Before the Fall

Before the Fall

Poems by

Mike Wilson

© 2026 Mike Wilson. All rights reserved.
This material may not be reproduced in any form, published,
reprinted, recorded, performed, broadcast,
rewritten or redistributed without
the explicit permission of Mike Wilson.
All such actions are strictly prohibited by law.

Cover design by Shay Culligan
Cover image by CJ on Unsplash
Hummingbird illustration by Ritam Baishya on Unsplash
Author photo by Bunny Wilson

ISBN: 979-8-90146-708-4

Kelsay Books
502 South 1040 East, A-119
American Fork, Utah 84003
Kelsaybooks.com

Acknowledgments

Some poems in this collection first appeared as indicated:

Amethyst Magazine: "Om"
The Avenue Journal: "Skinny-dip"
Bamboo Hut: "Staring Contest"
The Bard Review: "Green-Eyed Monster"
Dissent: "War"
Dust Poetry Magazine: "Little Wounds"
Encore: Prize Poems 2023 (National Federation of State Poetry Societies, 2023): "Nothing to Do But Climb," "Spring Passing"
Feed the Holy: "Instructions"
Green Ink: "Quietly in the Rain"
Hamilton Stone Review: "Ancestor Worship"
Heart: "Saturday"
Main Street Rag: "Bhakti"
Mockingheart Review: "We, Too," "Your Letter"
One Hand Clapping: "My Bindle"
The Poet: "We Leave the Lights On"
Pure Slush: "I Should Have Been a Better Friend"
The Queens Review: "Time Is Space Being Demolished"
The Rumen: "Spring Melic"
Turnpike Magazine: "Guileless Salaryman"
Willawaw Journal: "Directions to Canaan," "Light Behind a Blind"

Contents

Saturday	13
Today's To-Do List	14
Bhakti	15
Grace and the Lions	16
Spring Melic	17
Spring Passing	18
Om	19
Turn, a Dream Poem	20
Skinny-Dip	21
Turtle Dove	22
Heedless and Electrified	23
Whirling Dervish	24
Never an Orphan	25
Instructions	26
Directions to Canaan	27
Unstruck Bell	28
I Should Have Been a Better Friend, a Dream Poem	29
War	30
Buddha Smiles	32
We, Too	33
Green-Eyed Monster	34
Your Letter	35
Ignorance is	37
Nothing to Do But Climb	38
We Leave the Lights On	39
Ancestor Worship	40
My Bindle	41
Quietly in the Rain	42
Random Act of Kindness	43
Light Behind a Blind	44

Staring Contest	45
Little Wounds	46
Dear God, Pimp My Ride	47
Guileless Salaryman	48
Time Is Space Being Demolished	49
The Event	50
Before the Fall	51

Saturday

There are no cloudy Saturdays—
Saturday shines from inside out,
warming even the coldest day.
Saturday is the omnipotent smile,
the overpowering grace
rescuing every droopy face.
Freed from the cage of
Monday through Friday,
not yet kneeling in Sunday's pew,
everything's possible on Saturday.

Vows repeatedly broken
spring up like crocuses.
Time expands until a
universe can be crammed
into a single afternoon.
Should we all ever learn
to love one another,
it will happen on a Saturday.

Saturday is recess and merry-go-rounds,
the day it's okay to eat dessert.
Heaven will be endless Saturdays
where Jesus cleans out the garage
Mary cooks a Christmas pie
and the Holy Ghost inflates us,
laughing and laughing.

Today's To-Do List

Polish the planets.
Dust the stars.

Measure the depth of shadows
to expose their two-dimensionality.

Cook the Last Supper
as if it is the first.

Cartwheel through meadows.
Somersault down hills.

Order a pizza
and see if it obeys.

Watch everything pop out
like a jack-in-the-box.

Blindfold past and future.
Sunbathe in my birthday suit.

Bhakti

Love spirals out of the ground
thicker than what it surrounds.

Love is bread and the mouth that eats it.

Love makes planets spin
and circle stars or wander to their Mecca.

Love holds up the sky like a spinning plate.

Each moment, love is felt in the fingertips
of every galaxy in space-time.

Love literally motors the universe.

Oh, person who reads this—
that's how important your love is.

Grace and the Lions

I walk with Grace
the black-haired girl with a skip in her gait
who explains tournament facts of this final
match:
     We can actually win.

It sinks in.
        Sap in my spine soars like Jack's
beanstalk, fills the entire sky.
                My team
is smarter than what awaits
and we speak with endless light.

I never passed through arena gates this way

     until today.

Spring Melic

Singing life is stirring in the ether,
marching March and wrangling April's sap,
sprouting buds and stomping bass in rooted
tree-time under spreading shout-green treble
symphonizing stanzas of bel canto
baby-making in the always world
never seen, despite our listening to its
swishing sundress in the shimmering sky
spritzing chlorophyllic smelling salts,
slobbering stunned minds with sloppy kisses,
belly-dancing, belly-laughing, throwing
open oubliettes to set us free.
Squirrels are racing crazy up a tree's
leafy branches inside you and me.

Spring Passing

A golden shovel poem after Basho

I recall how the heartthrob of spring
leaps with hope catching fire and passes
quickly through veins of everything into the
ever-reaching green, beats in the wings of birds
courting, how their speckled eggs crack with a cry
declaring all miracles are effortlessly made out
of nothing but love, that all laughter and tears
are breath-blown spheres living forever in
etheric skies as satellites circling the
cooling star of surprise who eyes
her creation with the smile of
summer's river full of fishes

Om

A string between my forehead
and my viscera is taut.
Love draws a bow across my heart.

Mind flutters,
reed in a saxophone
of honey and brandy.

Blood pulses in time, they say.
I say,
> *What's this thing called time?*

Motion that carries a tune

Turn, a Dream Poem

Reclined in beach chairs eating ice cream
outside the insurance company's office by
the ocean.

The agent runs inside to get more ice cream.

My wife suggests I turn my chair
to face the ocean.

No! A wave might paw me into the sea!

I turn.

The sun is wonderfully blinding.
The blue-green bear gathers me in its arms.

Skinny-Dip

Pen in hand
slide inside

write a poem
trigger tremors

in my chest
levee breaks

sobbing gushing torrents rushing
slowing
motion

notion
swallowed in ocean

pen floats away

I sink
forever
in your arms
dear lifeguard who saves by drowning.

Turtle Dove

Divine Intervention,
crawl in the sack with me

Tonight's the night to be explicit
about illicit affairs

I've nothing to say of feathers and fur
or karmic obligations.

I'm turning down the covers.
The ball is in your court.

Heedless and Electrified

this lithe body
animated by voltage of desire

wriggles in
the ocean of immediacy

wrapping tentacles of want
around what it can reach

expressing
the human condition

Whirling Dervish

Reach for me in the present tense.
Our hands clasp, we emerge
in a womb where there's so much room.

Look for me in the eye of the hurricane.
Life and death roar and circle around
but we are perfectly still.

Listen for me in the silence
where stories start and finish together
and the middle never ends.

Smell me in the heavens of your heart
where I sit on a throne and hold a bouquet
of lavender for you.

I am the taste already on your tongue.
Gobble me like a greedy bee
until you swallow yourself.

Never an Orphan

putting my dreams to bed, these tired
children who breathe on their own but
depend on me to feed them
                                      defenseless
face on the pillowcase, closed eyes see
where the holy ghost goes
                                      and follow
the train of the queen's wedding dress

their little dream eyes open each morning
refreshed by the sponge bath of mercy
angels give in darkness
                              step
into daylight swollen with hope
not knowing they're only dreams
but sometimes in waking sleep I see
I am a dream
                       wondering who dreams me

Instructions

Think hologram
Conjure clouds of mist
that breathe

Be two places at once
Sense swimming synchronously
with your doppelganger

Open and close your eyes
Make room for something to happen
Make a place for parachutes to land

Directions to Canaan

Passports from other worlds
are used to travel this one
passports issued in foreign tongues
unheard by ordered understanding
whisper to sleepers in forgotten dreams.

Oh Holy Subconscious!
                            To Thee I bow,
Sustainer of the game, Your rules curving
out of reach, creating a miracle of trust,
each creature treading earth's crust
a satellite of the center miles below.

Two poles and a swing between—
a sign, if only we knew.

Unstruck Bell

Gentle rain made Sunday morning still,
made my tortured prisoner leap from his chair,
rubbing his wrists, ropes cut, but suffering
still draped across his shoulders like a habit,

draped across his shoulders like a boxer's robe
dropping when the bell sounds and he steps
into the ring with fear and desire in his chest,
into a drunken brawl that no one wins.

Pray, save this man from his own mind.
Let him dwell in the land of the unstruck bell.

I Should Have Been a Better Friend,
a Dream Poem

You're different—
still self-contained, manly,
but wrecked, like your mother.
Yet tidy as feminine hygiene.

You wear ear studs
but they look like thumb tacks.
I can't tell if it's fashion or medicine.
If I ask, you'll see it as intrusive
so I don't, but you want me to.

You are telling me something.
I hear words.
What you don't say is louder.
What you don't say is a cloud.
No one lives there but you.

You've always been this way,
a gruff saint concealing sacred sorrow.
But something brings you to me, now,
defenseless in a dream.
Something's changed in you,
and changed in me.

War

When the funneling tail finally touches ground,
choose an object of concentration.
                              First, eat.
Second, don't plan to die. Third, press your ear
against a seashell to hear each little anger's wave
combine with other angry waves into a tsunami.

Why are we surprised tsunamis seek a shore?
How are we surprised human hands
join to form a senseless punching fist?

                          *

War is warped cooperation, a gang smashing

                life
    liberty
                      property

War instills thrills of willfulness cloaked in ideals
feigning nobility but pivoting in selfishness.

Chests tighten, turbines behind breastbones spin
defense to offense, lies to truth, till everything has
as its only purpose the battering of its opposite.

*

War is a pod of orcas leaping, mortars launching
speeding with purpose at boats of blood
in a sea without a harbor.

War's older than dirt, ugliness so beautiful it
shatters mirrors, an erection unable to orgasm,
the crazy uncle escaping out of our basement.

War beats in a pickpocket's feet
snaps shut in a briefcase behind a wall of lawyers
does jumping jacks in a schoolyard bully's laugh
wiggles in a molester's tender eyes.

War is shadow demanding its season.

Buddha Smiles

I honor countless Buddha faces!
Every living creature is my intimate friend.
It is impossible that I should not help them.
It is impossible that they should not help me
in eons before and eons yet to come.
Oh, joyous universe
that even in remorseless killing
is nothing but loving-kindness!

We, Too

Stabbed by the bully with a paper clip:
"Bobby, what happened?"   *Nothing.*

Stabbed by the bully, this time with scissors:
"Bobby, what happened?"   *Nothing.*

"Bobby are you alright?"
I'm trapped in a dream.

Bobby can't find his body.
If he could, he'd choke it to death.

Fractals and fractions swell the room.
All the doors are locked.

The implications are ominous.
I don't want to live like this.

"None of us do, Bobby,
and our numbers are legion."

Green-Eyed Monster

I hate you for having something I don't,
even though I don't much want what you have,
hate my ungenerosity that won't
rejoice in your blessings. Where is the salve
to soothe this urge to destroy what glitters
in your hand? This hole in my heart, champagne
of conceit, hard cocktail of sweet bitters
blessed with a wicked kick knifing my brain,
crossing my eyes, birthing a ball of snakes
in my belly, vile bile, corkscrew twisted
by my own fisted fury. For God's sake!
Who knew, in me, such villainy existed?
But then, sprouting from frontal vanity
a seed that swallows greed—humility.

Your Letter

I

You write with barbed wire in your gut
a seven-layer salad of passive-aggression

your letter a curse hurled from a hurricane
bursting at the seams with blows below the belt

not seeing something inside you subpoenas
unhappiness to break bread with your own

writing *I won't hold on to negativity* in cursive
radioactive with a half-life longer than your own

your letter is a poisoned handkerchief
I drop from my hand too late—your venom

swims my veins like bootleg chemotherapy
this cocktail concocted from your own juices

delivered with mixed messages of a predator
luring someone into a windowless shack

II

Wrath aerates your platitudes like bubbles
hurtling to the surface of a pond.

I tread slowly and blind on your tar baby shores
making myself still and small and careful

balancing time like a tray about to topple
and spill tragedy on white linen tablecloths.

Your letter was a stage whisper I cannot hear
to prompt lines I won't recite and now

you're hiding behind a curtain where
the audience imagines your finger in the dike

a high school drama of scorn and salvation
Christ betrayed and alone until

God approaches during intermission
to share a cigarette in the garden.

Ignorance is

the enormous effort
we make to not see
everything
is one thing,
to deny that I am you and you are me,

the labor of building half-told tales
eliciting movement through their incompleteness.

Here's a trick to show you what I mean:

Freeze-frame any image.
Study it.

See how meaning emerges
through the movement of your mind?

Nothing to Do But Climb

I'm paid to hurl quarters from a tower
three hundred feet high
at a cancer below I locate by feeling
an itchy mole.
                      When I get vertigo,
I come down. Everyone's furious
because they bet money on it, *not*
because they want cancer cured.

Word on the street is each walks inside
the bubble of his or her very own dream
complaining
                 "Individual existence is *sooo*
exhausting! It requires *all* of your attention
and you're constantly being interrupted by
the existence of others!"

Interrupted, but just enough to toss and turn,
groping the dark for covers
the covers-hog dragged away.

It's four a.m.
I sip coffee, hand on the ladder.
The lower hemispheres are still.
There's nothing to do but climb.

We Leave the Lights On

I rise in darkness of the unformed day
drift to our living room, where my hand
reaching for the light switch is arrested
by the sight of Christmas tree lights—
blue and red, purple, yellow, green,
a burning cone of silent stars steering
hope past shoals we cannot see
in these strange seas of uncertainty
to what we need this Christmas to be

Ancestor Worship

We didn't take Christmas wreaths
to our parents' graves this year;
the ground housing their remains
is unvisited, unadorned.

Graves we visit hourly are
regrets and remembered loss,
the not-gotten gain we husband at
the lip of the black hole till we fall in

and join forgotten lives in ground
mowed by strangers, marked by stone
more steadfast than family, visited daily
by birds, at night by the wind.

My Bindle

One moment of intimacy
is longer than a decade of alone.

When I gave you everything
                            it became mine
but when I thought *mine*
                         I lost everything

except a bindle I shoulder
to haul my wounded imagination

Quietly in the Rain

the earth and I
huddle together
bubbled in a moment

of neon green
May screaming
screaming like a mime.

When silence is
that loud
I am comforted

before returning
to the madhouse
to serve out my sentence

Random Act of Kindness

smaller than a quark, bigger than infinity
this lightning bug in February twinkles

        steady on
        steady off
        steady on

lifts every heavy thing without muscles
settles my senses in easygoing anarchy

this directionless fly
                      buzzing
 yes
                yes
      yes

a stand-alone answer shushing all questions

Light Behind a Blind

Behind a blind a light switched on—
too dim for me to see
who stirred upstairs before the dawn
and rose invisibly.

Did the sleeper face the day
unwillingly, with dread—
or race past clock time, keen to say
the song inside her head?

Our parts are just our history
but—still—we read them cold.
Deep into this mystery—
what light could crack the mold?

Worm-wise warblers tweet and twerk
the news—pellucent Spring!
We fly by faith—it's always worked—
like them, we flap our wings.

Staring Contest

I eyeball God.
God eyeballs me.
Who'll blink?
Either way, my heart will break.

Little Wounds

They're flying drones, not kites
in the March afternoon park
where I exercise my soul

No diamond-faced sailors
chest-bumping urgent wind
blowing in renewal from Gaia

Just winged plastic, microchip
sensors, stringless humming
switchblades slicing air

Dear God, Pimp My Ride

I strip-search predawn song of a bird
for a word not a note of regret but truly
I have my fingers in my ears I hear only
lying tales of greed's grievance and the
slosh of sloth in my echo chamber
                              Lord!
Contemplate me in your divine car wash,
lead me under Your take-charge brushes,
swipe my grime, buffeth my bumpers,
Windex my windshield until it sparkles
that I may roll with the hope of a Trans Am
and steer with steady eyes of a Rolls Royce.

Guileless Salaryman

I'm throwing a retirement party
for my mind!

Congrats on years of loyal service
sending me on fool's errands
with a cookie in my lunchbox
and sorting lies with earnest eyes.

Here's your gold watch—
its pinwheel hands
marshal the aircraft of time
to the right runway.

Now you can lean back in your chair
on a porch somewhere
and let sunset and dawn
be one in your rheumy eyes.

Time Is Space Being Demolished

A jagged fracture in freeze-dried land
between now   and   a moment ago
defines   divides
          dares me to cross
         hurries me—pick quick!
        past is a building collapsing

I run   leap
           roof to roof
        never catch my breath

The Event

One day everybody woke up
and they didn't have to do this anymore.

The dead horse no longer needed beating.
Firemen stopped sniffing for smoke.

No one put on lipstick.
Plows stopped moving mid-furrow.

The starving children stopped starving.
The eating children stopped eating.

Airplanes hung like question marks in the sky
and all destinations vanished.

Not a tweet was heard, not even from birdies.
All passwords and birthdays were forgotten

and the edge of the universe expanded
faster than the eye could follow.

Some called it the Second Coming, but it was
more like a door opening with a *whoosh!*

Before the Fall

Hawaii calls—
we float in little boats
wearing comfortable clothes

We strum the ukulele
freely sing and touch each other
easy as the breeze

About the Author

Mike Wilson's work has appeared in many magazines and in his book, *Arranging Deck Chairs on the Titanic* (Rabbit House Press). His awards include the League of Minnesota Poets Award, Maine Poets Society Award, and Chaffin/Kash Prize of the Kentucky State Poetry Society. He lives in Lexington, Kentucky with his wife.

www.ingramcontent.com/pod-product-compliance
Lightning Source LLC
Chambersburg PA
CBHW031639160426